Jack B. Rollins has a Ph.D. in psychology and extensive experience in the academic world. He was raised in the Deep South in a rural environment where his life experiences and observations gave him a good perspective on a way of life unfamiliar to many.

Jack B. Rollins

REDNECK RHYMES AND OTHER POETIC THOUGHTS

AUSTIN MACAULEY PUBLISHERS™
LONDON • CAMBRIDGE • NEW YORK • SHARJAH

Ordering Information:
Quantity sales: special discounts are available on quantity purchases by corporations, associations, and others. For details, contact the publisher at the address below.

Publisher's Cataloging-in-Publication data
Rollins, Jack B.
Redneck Rhymes and Other Poetic Thoughts

ISBN 9781645755357 (Paperback)
ISBN 9781645755364 (Hardback)
ISBN 9781645755371 (ePub e-book)

Library of Congress Control Number: 2020917926

www.austinmacauley.com/us

First Published (2020)
Austin Macauley Publishers LLC
40 Wall Street, 28th Floor
New York, NY 10005
USA

mail-usa@austinmacauley.com
+1 (646) 5125767

I'd like to express my deep appreciation to my good friend, Nancy Sackman, whose initiative and diligence led to the publication of this book. Without her hard work and persistence, it would never have been published.

Table of Contents

Identification

Just how do you know, when a redneck's around?
They're almost everywhere, and easily found.
They're really not hard, to identify,
on the following clues, you can always rely.
A big four wheeler, that's jacked up a lot,
is the type of truck, most rednecks have got.
Big off-road tires, and a hitch in the back,
and usually they have, an inside gun rack.
Most drop out of school, at about the eighth grade,
their leavin' was due, to the grades that they made.
But endin' their schoolin', wasn't bad back then,
they could spell a few words, and count up to ten.
And sometimes their teeth, don't look just right,
both of them look, more brown than white.
You won't find a redneck, at a country club dance,
a museum or a lecture, nary a chance.
And a redneck won't go, to an opera or play,
for them that would be, a waste of a day.
The kind of event, where they spend their bucks,
is a big tractor pull, or some big wheel trucks.
But the next time you visit, a WalMart store,
just look down the aisles, you'll see them galore.

But to really find rednecks, the best place by far,
is at the car races, dirt track or Nascar.

Different

Growin' up in the country, I happened to see,
that many other folks, ain't just like me.
It's very apparent, in our human race,
that folks ain't too even, a fact we must face.
People are different, we can see right away,
as different as night time, is from the day.
Some people have bellies, as flat as can be,
it's cut and it's lean, with no fat to see.
But mine hangs over, my belt like a sack,
and when I bend over, you see a large crack.
Some have white teeth, they glisten and shine,
quite a contrast, to my friends' and mine.
Our teeth are unusual, a sight rarely seen,
a beautiful brown, with a slight tinge of green.
But I've got some things, which I think are best,
tattoos on my arm, my legs and my chest.
And my girlfriend's front's, as big as can be,
I don't know the size, but I guess triple D.
Now others are different, it's easy to see,
it's hard to be perfect, just like you and me.

Weddings

A big fancy weddin's, a marvelous affair,
for young 'uns to legally, join up as a pair.
This wedding was like, a big family meet,
all the guests were related, that was real neat.
This bride and groom, were made for each other,
she was marrying the son, of her older brother.
The cutest of couples, that you've ever seen,
'cause he's twenty-nine, she's almost fifteen.
And durin' the day, while he works his trade,
she's learning three Rs, in the school's seventh grade.
The girls wore long dresses, and perfumes like fruits,
most guys had on jeans, but a few leisure suits.
The bride's hair had ringlets, just recently set,
and held in position, with a coat of spray net.
The groom's boots were polished, had a bright shine,
and a crease in his jeans, ironed straight in a line.
A great big reception, and great food was served,
for this gourmet meal, a thanks was deserved.
With possum and chitlins, and deep fried coon,
I knew that my plate, I'd fill up real soon.
I piled my plate high, and put it on my lap,
after eatin' all that, I could sure use a nap.

For any earthly person, to cook such a meal,
a recipe from heaven, they had to steal.
So nobody choked, and to wash down the food,
and to help folks get into, a partying mood.
A keg of Blue Ribbon, sat iced in the sink,
and some red Solo cups, to use when you drink.
Besides the cold beer, they had some White Lightnin',
too much of this, the results can be frightenin'.
A blue grass band played, until early morn,
the last song they played, was "Shucking the Corn".
The newlyweds left, at the very last sound,
it's honeymoon time, they're Dollywood bound.

Teeth

I woke up one mornin', my jaw hurt real bad,
I thought it was caused, by the Busch that I had.
I'd drunk several bottles, the night before,
lucky I ran out, or I would have had more.
I realized later, that the cause of my pain,
was a half rotten tooth, that was hurtin' again.
So I went to the dentist, later in the day,
and asked him to please, make the pain go away.
He took out a needle, and gave me a shot,
so pulling the tooth, wouldn't hurt a whole lot.
He put on thick glasses, 'cause he couldn't see well,
started pulling and yanking, and it hurt like Hell.
With this tooth pulled out, I thought we'd be done,
but the half blind dentist, had pulled the wrong one.
For this bad mistake, I wasn't too unhappy,
'cause I've still got three teeth, one more than my Pappy.

Camping

I wanted a camper, big and fancy but used,
so I bought a newspaper, and the ads I perused.
For the campers I liked, I couldn't afford to pay,
so I figured I'd have to go, some other way.
Then I went down the street, to the RV store,
made an offer on one, they wanted much more.
So I thought why not, just build myself one?
I know what to do, to get it all done.
Getting things that I need, shouldn't be hard,
just pick up some parts, at the local junk yard.
I found a tin shed, what a great piece of luck,
and I bolted it down, to the back of my truck.
I put an old mattress, on the floor of the shed,
this made a real comfortable, two person bed.
Inside I built shelves, up high on one side,
I could now put my stuff, up safely inside.
My cooler is one thing, I like to keep near,
I hoped its weight, the new shelves would bear.
I filled it with Busch, and a whole bunch of ice,
I can get to it easy, which is real real nice.
In the top of the shed, I put in a fan,
to cool the inside, as much as I can.

The hole for the fan, really lets the air flow,
but the rain keeps wettin', the things down below.
But I won't let this problem, ruin my fun,
I'll only go camping, when there's lots of sun.
My camper's got dents, and a good bit of rust,
I don't really care, it's still "Florida or Bust".

Speed

I work very hard, 'til late every day,
gettin' all that I can, from overtime pay.
My wife does the same, nary a complaint,
this hard working lady, is truly a saint.
She paints lots of nails, and does pedicures,
and never complains, she just endures.
We save all our money, and drive an old car,
and never go out, to a restaurant or bar.
Our house is real small, in need of revision,
our only entertainment, is an old television.
But life ain't as dreary, as it seems to be,
'cause one time a year, we go on a spree.
February's cold, up in these here hills,
so we always leave, to avoid these chills.
We rent us a camper, and stock it with beer,
and we aim to the South, and put it in gear.
We've only one goal, we know what we seek,
it's Daytona Beach, for their annual speed week.
We're drivin' real fast, so we won't get there late,
we already bought tickets, to get in the gate.
When we get to Daytona, there's thousands of fans,
there's pickups and campers, and all kinds of vans.

We go thru the tunnel, and get parked inside,
there's more trucks and campers, some double wide.
We buy us some flags, and decals and such,
and a bobble-head Dale, it didn't cost much.
We plaster our camper, with the big number eight,
to show we think Junior, is really first rate.
We grab a cold Busch, and head toward the pits,
'cause sometimes that's, where King Richard sits.
"Start your engines", we suddenly hear,
and we know the racin', is now really near.
And just as we hear, the engines' loud roar,
the sky opens up, and the clouds start to pour.
The rains didn't stop, for nearly a week,
this wasn't the pleasure, that we came to seek.
But you can drink beer, without any sun,
so that's what we did, and had lots of fun.
We bought lots of trinkets, spent most of our cash,
and we plan to come back, for next year's bash.

Hounds

I wanted a dog, so I went to the pound,
in one of the cages, was a Blue Tic hound.
He's exactly the dog, I wanted to see,
so I paid his fine, and took him with me.
Now I'm real disappointed, I have to say,
'cause all he does, is sleep all the day.
I call him "Useless", but that ain't his name,
his real name is "Eustis", they sound 'bout the same.
Some say he's dumb, and some say he's crazy,
but in my opinion, he's just plain lazy.
You'd think he would hunt, being a hound,
but he'll only hunt, for food that's around.
And as a retriever, he ain't very good,
anything he retrieves, he uses for food.
My neighbor's got a dog, he calls her "Smelly",
that ain't her real name, her real name is "Nellie".
She's just like "Useless", ain't worth a hoot,
he took her duck huntin', she chased down a Coot.
The "Coot" that she chased, dragged her back to him,
cause "Nellie" never bothered, to learn how to swim.
If these two should mate, and a family get started,
their pups would be lazy, and surely retarded.

Girlfriend

My girlfriend Irene, is a true gift of gold,
a startling beauty, for all to behold.
She's five foot tall, and a real sight to see,
this solid build girl, weighs one-eighty-three.
With red shiney lips, and if you look below,
the reflected light, makes her belly ring glow.
With several earrings, lined up on one ear,
her ear's really smaller, than it would appear.
She wears pointed shoes, with long spiked heels,
with blue jeans so tight, God knows how it feels.
She's a quadruple "D", with a chest like that,
it's gotta be implants, supplemented with fat.
This week she's a blond, all over her head,
but last week her hair, was a very bright red.
Her long curved nails, a manicurist's delight,
are all painted red, and a red very bright!
On her arms are tattoos, one arm says "mother",
a heart pierced with arrows, covers the other.
What a great girl she is, for me such a dream,
she's got lots to love, with her very wide beam.

Autos

I've got an old Chevy, parked out in my yard,
I've wanted to move it, but the job seemed too hard.
It really belongs, to my second ex-wife,
she moved out and left it, to start a new life.
If she'd tried to take it, it wouldn't be easy,
with parts strewn all over, all dirty and greasy.
And the tires are gone, so it don't roll too good,
and the wheels are jacked up, on a big piece of wood.
It don't bother nobody, and it just sits out there,
and without any tires, it ain't goin' nowhere.
But accordin' to the County, it's contamination,
and they threatened to give me, a code violation.
I can't understand why, they get so upset,
I worked on it last year, but it ain't fixed yet.
I can't really junk It, 'cause it ain't really mine,
but if I don't do somethin', I'm gonna' get a fine.
I need to do something, just as fast as I can,
but I think that I have it, a really good plan.
If I let all the weeds, grow up tall and thick,
nobody could see it, that'd do the trick.
I'll let the weeds grow up, taller than me,
they'll think the car's gone, 'cause it they can't see.

But I hope at my house, they don't look out back,
my old pickup truck's, sitting there on a jack.

Home

The place where I live, that where I reside,
is my mobile home palace, and it's double wide.
To keep it from gettin', too hot inside,
I've air conditioned, my big double wide.
I attached to the front, a porch that I made,
it's got a tin roof, to provide needed shade.
The dirt floor I covered, with discarded rugs,
and screened in the sides, to keep out the bugs.
I put my food smoker, just outside the door,
so the smoked Mullet juice, won't drip on the floor.
And inside my home, I've got a TV,
it's a fifty inch screen, real easy to see.
The antenna's mounted, above the front door,
it gets me three channels, and sometimes four.
Just outside the door, is a big packing crate,
it's a home for Ol' Blue, boy does he rate!
Off to the side, and way out of the way,
my old pickup sits, I'll fix it someday.
And in the front yard, is a big metal drum,
to burn all my trash, my place ain't no slum.
Not far from this drum, I happened to see,
a mower I had left there, in about '03.

Home (Continued...)

It's lookin' real bad, all dirty and rusted,
I left it right there, when its engine busted.
To improve the landscape, I planted some flowers,
I hope they'll get watered, by afternoon showers.
I found my old sprinkler, it worked really swell,
but the hose that I had, wouldn't reach the well.
Some flowers are in tires, and some are in pots,
I put garbage around them, they'll grow when it rots.
I planted my flowers, from the house far away,
so I can't smell the garbage, as it starts to decay.
The smell ain't too bad, I've smelled worse before,
when my dry well backed up, and flooded the floor.
My home may be simple, and not much to see,
but I really like it, it's a mansion to me.
There're two other things, in which I take pride,
my Confederate flag, really tickles my hide.
And the sign in the yard, that I think is neat,
says, "y'all come back soon, Gladys and Pete."

Hunters

For most of the year, in my community,
I try to do good, with much impunity.
I'm a true blue pillar, of society,
a model of goodness, and sobriety.
I go to my job, each and every day,
I work real hard, and bring home my pay.
I rarely do things, that are very wild,
I'm in church on Sunday, with wife and child.
When someone needs help, I'm up to the task,
I rush to their aid, as soon as they ask.
I donate my time, without any pause,
and always help, with any good cause.
I go to funerals, when someone dies,
and other occasions, when they arise.
But when Fall approaches, I start acting strange,
and people observe, in me a big change.
My attention to others, has faded away,
I appear to be focused, on some other day.
What could be wrong, what is the reason?
Why this change, in this pre-winter season?
Now all those things, that I used to do,
must take a back seat, for a month or two.

The only thing now, that'll bring me a thrill,
is hiding and stalking, and making the kill.
I keep on hoping, I'll have some good luck,
and get me a six, or an eight point Buck.
After much male bonding, and drinking of beer,
I finally head home, with the meat of a deer.
Once I get home, and put away my gear,
I'm already thinking, ahead to next year.
For the next few months, it's easy to see,
I'm right back just, like I used to be.

Drawl

The beautiful sounds, that flow from your mouth,
are unique to those, who grew up in the South.
It's spoken real slowly, much like a slow crawl,
what I'm talking about, is our Southern drawl.
In the movies they attempt, to imitate it,
but it's real poorly done, if I had to rate it.
"You all" two words, they typically say,
when "y'all", one word, is the true Southern way.
And in the South we don't often, enunciate,
it's not part of the way, we communicate.
"Rs" at the end, of a word we don't say,
ending words with "AH", is the Southern way.
In "daughter" and "water", the "R" ain't pronounced,
to end words in "R", in the South is denounced.
The occasional "ain't", you'll sometimes hear,
means that a Southern, redneck is near.
Sometimes in our drawl, and it might sound moronic,
the words that you hear, sound a little ebonic.
But my favorite thing, that Southerners say,
they pronounce different words, all the same way.
They pronounce just alike, the words "bear" and "beer",
and also the same with "dare", "dear", and "deer".

They say the same way, the words "air" and "ear",
and rhyming with these, are the words "fare" and "fear".
Now this doesn't mean, our accent is broken,
'cause we understand, these words as they're spoken.
Maybe our way of speakin', sounds funny to some,
but it ain't gonna change, for a long time to come.

Closet

Most rednecks tend to be alike, and act pretty much the same.
Most have a truck with great big tires, and a very flashy dame.
Some have tattoos on their arms, and usually they act tough.
Their manners sometimes ain't too pretty, and often pretty rough.
I grew up as a true redneck, and I like the things they do,
like drinkin' Busch at tractor pulls, and at auto races too.
Country music really turns me on, and I like Garth and Willie,
I'm so excited when I hear it, I laugh and act real silly.
I've got guns and rods and reels, and other grown up toys,
and one of my favorite things to do, is huntin' with the boys.
But I'm quite different from the others, in you I must confide,
sometimes my judgment fails me, and I show my effeminate side.
At sporting events I cheer real hard, and raise my arms and fist,
but I see as I raise my arm, I have a slight limp wrist.
I'm a forty year old bachelor, very neat and very trim,

there're always lots of girls around, but I'd rather be with
him.
My life is so much easier now, since I don't have to hide.
I'm glad I'm out of the closet, and I'll never go back inside.
I still have all the friends I had, I'm pleased as pink to say,
but now they call me Brucie, our friend the redneck gay.

Swamps

I'm hopin' tonight, I'll have me some luck,
I hooked my boat trailer, to the back of my truck.
I pumped up the tires, 'cause the air leaks out slow,
then I tested my motor, I didn't want to row.
My old Jon boat's ready, it works really well,
'cept the rivets are loose, so it leaks like Hell.
I got my head light, and the rest of my riggin',
now down to the swamp, for a night of frog giggin'.
With the light on my head, tied like a bandana,
I'm ready to go gig, Rana Catesbeiana.
Now this fancy word, it's just another name,
for a big bullfrog, it really means the same.
When you go giggin', in the swamp late at night,
much danger is lurkin', mostly out of sight.
If you do somethin' dumb, or make a mistake,
you'll likely encounter, a big scary snake.
As the night passes on, either sooner or later,
you'll probably meet up, with a big alligator.
Now don't make an error, and gig this big boy,
he'll turn your boat over, like a small water toy.
You should gig only frogs, just take this advice,
if you gig only frogs, you won't pay the price.

If your aim is real true, and you get a whole bunch,
you can eat 'em for dinner, leftovers for lunch.
If you fry 'em up right, they'll be finger lickin',
and the best part is, they taste just like chicken.

Proud

There's really no doubt, she's one of a kind,
the type that you hoped, you'd someday find.
When I take her out, for the public to see,
I fear that admirers, will steal her from me.
I hear many comments, both whispers and loud,
they make me feel good, and certainly proud.
But the things that really, mean most to me,
are the things naked eyes, can't usually see.
She purrs like a kitten, and runs like a top,
has pretty good brakes, to bring her to a stop.
She sometimes runs hot, makes the radiator boil,
and smokes quite a bit, 'cause she uses some oil.
She's jacked up real high, way up off the ground,
the muffler's got a hole, and makes a loud sound.
The tires are real big, some cheap off-road brand,
but perfect for muddin', and goin' thru sand.
She's got a few dents, and the doors don't match,
the tailgate stays down, 'cause it ain't got a latch.
But this little truck, is just perfect for me,
This "79 Diesel", by the great GMC.

Excitement

The week is all gone, and I'm real excited,
'cause it's Saturday night, and I've been invited.
By some real nice folks, to a fancy affair,
and I'll take along my wife, so we'll be a pair.
My jeans are all washed, my boots really shine,
I've gotta look good, at a shindig this fine.
There's gonna be music, and plenty to drink,
and I'm gonna bathe, 'cause I don't wanna stink.
I'll wear my new cap, the bill to the rear,
so the Walmart logo, is seen really clear.
It ain't too often, that I get included,
is this really happenin', or am I deluded?
As things get started, there's a race of my heart,
when I hear the first sound, of a big Diesel start.
The stadium erupts, from the stands that are full,
at the county's first annual, big tractor pull.

Repairs

My home's getting old, and it ain't much to see,
I could fix it up, or just let it be.
It don't bother me, I think it looks fine,
my wife don't agree, and continues to whine.
She's always complainin', it don't look too good,
so I fixed the front door, even put in new wood.
But the roof still sags, and has a small leak,
she wants me to fix it, before the storms peak.
If you click the switch, for the light in the hall,
the stove starts to work, and the fan in the wall.
Just one more problem, for her to complain,
I fix and repair, but never seem to gain.
To make her happy, and make things look neat,
I painted one day, in the afternoon heat.
The heat brought the rain, got everything wet,
and the paint washed off, before it could set.
It don't look too good, running down the side,
of my beautiful home, my big double wide.
If I started over, painted all you can see,
she might quit yelling, and just let me be.
I doubt this would work, 'cause the toilet's still broke,
the way that it flushes, to me is a joke.

When nature calls, and you go in for a set,
the spray shoots up, and gets you all wet.
I offered to build her, a privy outside,
somethin' brand new, for our old double wide.
She didn't like that, and the idea rejected,
she cried and she said, that she felt neglected.
My future I fear, is now very clear,
constant complaints, are all I will hear.
To stop these complaints, too much is required,
all must be fixed, and the whole house rewired.
Should I do these things, to please my sweet wife,
or hear her complain, the rest of my life.
To deal with this problem, is a real big decision,
but suddenly my mind, experienced a vision.
Don't fix anything, put everything on hold,
and trade in my wife, for a twenty-year-old.

Reunion

My wife's big reunion, is getting really near,
since my trailer's bigger, I host it each year.
To see all the family, I'm excited and elated,
lots of folks are comin', and all of them related.
My uncle Clemmy's bringin', his second wife Dee,
she's uncle Ferd's daughter, pretty as can be.
Uncle Ferd is comin' too, his wife at his side,
many years ago, she was uncle Clemmy's bride.
Aunt Gert and her two sons, surely will arrive,
their IQs ain't too high, and both are named Clive.
It might seem confusin', with both names the same,
but not too confusin', with a different last name.
Cousin Olive will come, if she fits thru the door,
the chairs won't hold her, so she sits on the floor.
Last year one time she tried, to sit in a chair,
it's now outside in the shed, in need of repair.
Aunts Irene and Ethyl, will each bring their brother,
one's married to Ethyl, and Irene to the other.
To prepare for the party, and be a good host,
I wanna get the food, that they like the most.
Armadillo and possum, are a real good fare,
but I'd have to go hunting, 'cause my freezer's bare.

Maybe some seafood, like gator tail or gar,
or pickled pig's feet, which I buy in a jar.
I worry too much, about being a good host,
and trying to decide, what they would like most.
With a keg of Blue Ribbon, and a jug of moonshine,
road kill or dog food, would suit them just fine.

Smokin'

Here in the hills where I grew up, everybody smoked,
on my first try I coughed a lot, and also nearly choked.
Many tries and years of practice, I got more proficient,
I only smoked two packs a day, which I felt was sufficient.
Health warnings printed on the pack, I chose to ignore,
I puffed and puffed my cigarettes, just like I'd done before.
I noticed changes as I smoked, the first thing that I found,
my teeth, always pearly white, now were turning brown.
I also noticed in my clothes, a strong smell seemed to linger,
and nicotine stains, ugly and brown, appeared on my finger.
Breath that always smelled real good, odorless and pure,
now took on an awful smell, much like horse manure.
Most think smokin's bad for you, says the many studies,
but it never really bothered me, or any of my buddies.
They all appeared pictures of health, healthy as can be,
and most of them lived long lives, at least to thirty-three.
My granddaddy, just like me, for many years he smoked,
he lived to be very old, but at forty-one he croaked.
I ain't changin', I ain't scared, by all of these health threats,
I'm gonna keep my habit, and enjoy my cigarettes.
I tried the new electric smokes, but they aren't up to par,
the taste you get ain't too good, no nicotine and tar.

Now my health is really good, I'm feelin' my very best,
I hardly notice the cough I have, or the fluid in my chest.
Sometimes I feel my heart flutter, and then it skips a beat,
I'm sure it's indigestion, and caused by the food I eat.
With my clean living and good health, a long life I will see,
I'm sure to outlive granddaddy, to maybe forty-three.

Boats

For most all of my life, I really liked to fish,
just catch 'em and fry 'em, they're really delish.
Shellcracker or Bream, or a big Mudcat,
all taste really great, "boy that's where it's at".
Sometimes with luck, you might get an eel,
or hook a small gator, that'll tear up your reel.
But the problem I have, I ain't got a boat,
I don't need nothin' fancy, just so it will float.
At the boat store prices, they looked really bad,
it'd take lots more cash, than I ever had.
And the ads in the paper, didn't help very much,
only yachts and sailboats, kayaks and such.
This search for a boat, was gettin' really hard,
'til one day I saw, a sign stuck in a yard.
A twelve foot boat, they were trying to sell,
sounds like a boat, that would suit me real well.
An aluminum Jon boat, one made by Sears,
it's a little beat up, but nobody really cares.
And a six horse Johnson motor, to push it along,
and to keep it moving, if the current is strong.
This boat seems perfect, I can't ask for more,
but then I noticed, there's a big hole in the floor.

My chances now of buying, just got very slim,
I wouldn't mind the hole, 'cept that I can't swim.
I'd have a real big problem, if my new boat sank,
so I'll have to keep on fishin', right off of the bank.

Haberdashery

I haven't bought clothes, for many a year,
and my wife says mine, have got lots of wear.
To make sure she's happy, I'll get me some more,
so off I go, to the haberdasher store.
I jumped in my truck, and gave her a start,
and took right out, for the local Walmart.
The store's really big, and I looked all around,
and the men's department, I finally found.
They had lots of pants, and shirts and such,
but none of them suited, my needs very much.
But I know a place, I've got clothes before,
the clothes I want, they've got 'em galore.
On this store I know, I can always rely,
and it's right down the street, the Tractor Supply.
I walked in the store, right past the feed,
to the aisle behind, where they sell the seed.
A couple of plows, I then walked around,
and the overall counter, was there to be found.
I bought me a pair, with adjustable bibs,
I can pull 'em up easy, right over my ribs.
But shopping ain't over, I need something more,
I might as well get it, in this fancy store.

My Long Johns are old, with stains and some tears,
but being under your clothes, nobody really cares.
The kind they were sellin', were the kind I wear,
buttons down the front, a trap door in the rear.
Now I'm feelin' real dapper, in my new overalls,
and the trap door's real handy, for when nature calls.

'Shine

I crept through the woods, past spiders and ants,
with Beggar Lice sticking, all over my pants.
I climbed up the hills, and crawled thru the ditches,
got dirty all over, and a rip in my britches.
Now what's so important, to make me endure,
this unpleasant task, it's not fun I'm sure.
It's the government's fault, I can so attest,
I'm forced to do this, to avoid my arrest.
I'm lookin' for a spot, not easily found,
'cause a revenooer might, be snoopin' around.
I wanna make 'shine, I know it's unlawful,
it's a real bad law, my friends think it's awful.
Everybody loves 'shine, up here in these hills,
I can make me some cash, to help pay the bills.
Real good 'shine ain't, too hard to make,
but you need lots of water, from a crick or a lake.
And a whole bunch of corn, to make up the mash,
the corn you can get, without too much cash.
You put the wet mash, in a big copper pot,
let it sit a few days, then heat it real hot.
And the steam as it rises, let none go to waste,
it soon turns to 'shine, with a wonderful taste!

Just drain the new 'shine, straight into a pail,
then put it in jars, if you ain't now in jail.
Don't tell no one where, you make your shine,
if the gov'ment finds out, it means a big fine.
If you like legal liquor, the stores have a lot,
but it'll cost more, than you've likely got.
But if you like 'shine, you can get it for free,
just come by my still, and get it from me.

Gourmet

Me and my buddy, wanted something to eat,
and we wanted a tasty, gourmet type treat.
We didn't want to make, a decision too hasty,
'cause we really wanted, a meal that was tasty.
We decided on 'coon, after much thought,
but 'coon ain't something, that's easily bought.
How to get a 'coon, without spending much dough?
We decided to hunt one, was the best way to go,
so we got out our rifle, and a good spotlight,
for 'coon you have, to hunt them at night.
We went out and saw one, in the top of a tree,
we didn't realize, how easy this would be.
We dispatched our prey, took it home to clean,
was the smelliest 'coon, that I've ever seen.
We were hunting at night, it was hard to see,
and a skunk our prey, turned out to be.
The next time we want, a real gourmet meal,
something else to us, I'm sure will appeal.
And it won't be a 'coon, I'm certain to say,
'cause armadillo tastes better, most folks say.

Hoosgow

The judge said, "Son, that'll be sixty days,
you'll now have time, to mend your bad ways."
I didn't do anything, that's really wrong,
'cept going out to bars, and staying too long.
Started early and into, the night I did stay,
drinking beer and spending, my whole month's pay.
This ain't too bad but, my ex-wife did complain.
that I owed alimony, hadn't paid it again.
Now jail ain't so bad, and I've been here before,
for fightin' with my wife, kicking down the door.
In jail you get three, great meals a day,
just go thru the line, and it's served on a tray.
You can bide your time, watchin' cable TV,
and it don't cost nothin', you get it for free.
And almost no work, just make up your cot,
this is better than home, in here what I've got.
So when I get out, I'll not pay my ex-wife,
and they'll put me back here, to live the good life.

Wealthy

I've got an idea, how we all can get rich,
we can use my old boat, now sunk in a ditch.
I got this idea, from some guy on TV,
and I thought that's a great, idea for me.
The person on TV, was a guy called Lefty,
he looked pretty tough, also a bit hefty.
I don't know how, he got this great harm,
but he was missing, his entire right arm.
He was driving a brand new, truck by Ford,
and was pulling a boat, that I can't afford.
How he made all his money, I think was neat,
he caught alligators, and then sold the meat.
And the skins also brought, him a good price,
from them they make shoes, real fancy and nice.
For us to get started, we won't need a lot,
'cause most of the stuff, I've already got.
Old fishhooks, some rope, and some kind of gun,
we'll hook 'em and shoot 'em, before they can run.
We can use my old boat, which is sunk in the ditch.
and then get to hunting, and we all get rich.
So the next time I see you, it should be no surprise,
when I ask you to be part, of my great enterprise.

Draggy

Too much bar hopping, and too much to drink,
makes your eyes go bad, I do really think.
'Cause back in my youth, as I seem to recall,
I was out chasing girls, and having a ball.
I found me a girl, the most perfect you'll see,
and she took an immediate, liking to me.
Her pearly white teeth, had a beautiful shine,
and a rear view revealed, a real great behind.
It was difficult for me, to not stare and gaze,
at her triple D breasts, which to me did amaze.
Her eyes were just gorgeous, a beautiful blue,
they would even look good, in some other hue.
Her face was fantastic, with a cute little nose,
and her pretty round cheeks, red like a rose.
So we're off to my place, after much persuasion,
I was really looking forward, to a great occasion.
But instead of great fun, I just faded away,
didn't wake up 'til early, the following day.
As I looked at that girl, in my bed still asleep,
the way she looked now, made me start to weep.
My vision got ruined, by the drinks I did buy.
'cause the person in bed, now looks like a guy.

Now my eyes are all well, like they used to be,
and everywhere I now go, I'm sure I will see,
only beautiful girls, none being a hag,
But I'll still make sure, they're not men in drag.

Sporty

In my earlier years, I tried lots of fishin',
but I never caught nearly, what I was wishin'.
So I bought lots of lures, a new rod and reel,
but I still didn't get, any fish in my creel.
I then took up bowling, I thought I'd be good,
but I did much worse, than I thought I would.
So I got bowling shoes, and a custom made ball,
but my scores got worse, and continued to fall.
So I then took up tennis, as a different sport,
but I couldn't make the ball, land in the court.
So I bought a new racquet, to improve my game,
but my terrible tennis, remained just the same.
So I started playing golf, it didn't look hard,
I took lots of lessons, and practiced in my yard.
But the balls that I hit, had a very poor flight,
some went to the left, and some to the right.
But I knew the problem, so new clubs I bought,
the ball should now go, where I think it ought.
But it still didn't do what, I thought it would do,
and it rarely went where, I tried to hit it to.
After buying all the new, golf clubs they sell,
my game was still bad, I didn't do very well.

What new activity, should I undertake now?
Something my athletic, skills will allow.
The sport that I chose, after lots of thinkin',
was one that I'm good at, beer and wine drinkin'.
No equipment is needed, I'm glad to report,
so I think that today, I'll start my new sport.
With lots of practice, one would assume,
lots more beer and wine, I could consume.

Calculations

Went fishin' one day, and caught me a bunch,
I cooked them and made, a sandwich for lunch.
I was thinkin' this sure, is a wonderful day,
got a great fish sandwich, didn't have to pay.
But I kept on thinkin', while my sandwich I ate,
as I thought my mind started, to calculate.
I had to buy gas, for my boat and my truck,
or somewhere real bad, I'll probably get stuck.
I spent fifty bucks, just for buyin' the gas,
I thought now I'm ready, to go for the Bass.
But then I remembered, I've got to buy bait,
so a few minutes longer, the fishin' must wait.
While buying the bait, the store's cooler was near,
so I bought me a six pack, of ice cold beer.
With beer I knew, that I needed a snack,
I bought nuts and chips, so food I'd not lack.
I'm glad I didn't have, to buy anything more,
'cause I spent thirty bucks, at the stupid bait store.
And my boat I remembered, ain't paid for yet,
at two hundred a month, the payments are set.
So I guess my fish sandwich, wasn't quite free,
nearly four hundred bucks, is what it cost me.

The next time I want, a fish sandwich to eat,
twenty bucks at the market, is real hard to beat.

Options

I've been smokin' Marlboros, most of my life,
since long before I, ever married my wife.
But now she insists, that I must quit smokin',
when she first said it, I thought she was jokin'.
She said smokin's costly, will use up my wealth,
and in addition she said, it'll ruin my health.
And she said that smokin', made my breath smell,
so I told her hers also, doesn't smell very well.
As far as her thinkin', my wealth's going away,
my EBT card pays for, my smokes every day.
Her concern for my health, she's just giving me lip,
'cause the coughin' I do's, from my post nasal drip.
My health's not a problem, it makes me real happy,
'cause in most every way, I'm just like my Pappy.
He smoked many years, and got along fine,
and he lived a long life, to almost forty-nine.
It's the biggest decision, I've made in my life,
do I give up my smokin', or get a new wife?
You'll soon know, what the answer will be,
just wait 'til the next time, that you see me.
Will it just be me, still puffin' and smokin',
or my wife sitting there, all happy and jokin'.

Well she'll there happy, as the day we were wed,
'cause I gave up smokin', started chewing instead.

Revenge

The life of a buzzard, must not be much fun,
he can't roller skate, swim, or go for a run.
His feathers the pretty, colors do lack,
no reds, no blues, just nothing but black.
All he does all day, is just soar around,
trying to spot carrion, dead on the ground.
But sometimes he'll have, a real lucky day,
and find some road kill, out on a highway.
But trying to eat it, he hasn't much luck,
he almost gets run over, by a car or a truck.
Time after time, he still gives it a try.
but the cars speeding by, makes him have to fly.
So the poor ugly bird, gets nothing to eat,
'cause the cars going by, repeat and repeat.
Now the ugly ole buzzard, is getting real mad,
the road kill's all squashed, and none has he had.
Now the buzzard is thinking, he'd get a big thrill,
paying back those cars, who ruined his kill.
So he flew up and lit, in the top of a tree,
right over where, a car's windshield will be.
He grunted and grunted, let out all his poop,
it covered the windshield, like runny old soup.

After messing the windshield, up really good,
he then moved out, now over the hood.
He grunted and strained, and pooped once again,
all over the hood, it came down like rain.
As a parting shot, he found a dead rat,
dumped it on the car, right where it sat.
Now all this won't make him, get more road kill,
but it did make him happy, and gave him a thrill.

Maturation

Sparkling blue eyes, and a smile that's so sweet,
those rosy red cheeks, and the cute little feet.
An innocent babe, as sweet as can be,
not a care in the world, it's easy to see.
With passage of time, many changes take place,
a teenager appears, with zits on his face.
His father gets angry, his mother sheds tears,
to see such a change, in just a few years.
From innocent child, to a boy who is rude,
a surly young man, with a bad attitude.
But don't give up hope, the change isn't done,
he'll be nice again, at about twenty-one.
Girls are the same, in the way that they act.
as teens they get bratty, and that is a fact.
They lock their room doors, and sit there alone,
playing loud music, talking on their phone.
Ask them a question, they act like they're mad,
never a nice word, for their mother or dad.
But do not despair, better things are in sight,
at roughly nineteen, most start acting right.

Versatility

It's interesting stuff, that you have on your head,
it continues to grow, even after you're dead.
It covers your body, almost everywhere,
except soles and palms, you won't find it there.
It possesses a number, of unusual features,
and is found on many, of Ma Nature's creatures.
It's colors are many, almost every hue,
it's red, blonde, and black, but not often blue.
It's straight or it's curly, and is sometimes seen,
colored orange or pink, or occasionally green.
Your head's not alone, where these sprouts grow,
they cover your body, from head to below.
You can cut it or curl it, or put it in a wave,
or straighten it or dye it, or give it a shave.
You brush it or comb it, or sometimes you set it,
you blow it, you dry it, and often you wet it.
People sometimes see it, as sexy and hot,
and some are unhappy, when they don't have a lot.
We take it for granted, think it won't go away,
and sometimes it doesn't, it just turns all gray.
If it starts falling out, as it frequently will,
you can make it grow back, with Monoxidil.

Its color, its length, nothing ever looks right,
but a body all bare, is a far worse sight.
It sometimes appears, in unwanted places,
like on ladies' legs, or on ladies' faces.
But this is alright, they shouldn't despair,
it's easily removed, with a small dab of Nair.
Some spend lots of cash, to make it look nice,
we're all somewhat guilty, of this little vice.

English

It's easy to see, why some foreign folks,
are often the brunt, of our silly jokes.
The English they speak, is frequently bad,
their pronouncing of words, truly is sad.
I guess that the reasons, are easy to see,
English words differ, from what they should be.
Why is the "ou", in a word like "cough",
pronounced in a way, that sounds like "off"?
While the same two letters, in a word like "through",
are always pronounced, like they rhyme with "glue".
And why are these letters, in a word like "ought",
most often pronounced, to rhyme with "taut"?
And the "ou" in "thou", is pronounced like "cow",
so why isn't "though" pronounced like "how"?
And a fat mama pig, is called a "sow",
and this word sounds, like "how" or "now".
But two different words, like "sew" and "sow",
are both pronounced, like they rhyme with "row".
To learn English right, one must be persistent,
'cause much of this language, is real inconsistent.

How do we know, it's the "wind" that will blow,
or a clock we'll "wind", so it won't run slow?
And we spell with an "i", when we're spelling "wind",
so why use an "e", when we're spelling "mend"?
In words like "Marseilles", we don't say the "l",
you must leave them silent, to pronounce it well.
But in most other words that, we use every day,
like "pallet" or "mullet", the "ls" we will say.
This language is tough, on that I won't dwell,
so I must be real smart, 'cause I speak it well.

Metamorphosis

No wrinkles or sags, and everything's tight,
no cellulite hips, and the weight's about right.
Buns just like steel, and breasts all erect,
a perfect young lass, just like you'd expect.
Most perfect white teeth, that you'll ever see,
all that you'd want, in a girl twenty-three.
But as the years come, and begin to go past,
at a rate I might add, that seems very fast.
The wrinkles appear, and her eyes start to bag,
the skin on her neck, and her arms starts to sag.
That perfect size body, that never gained a pound,
has rapidly grown, and is now very round.
The fat cells are filling, from her head to her feet,
adding pounds to her body, and much cellulite.
Her pretty white teeth, and her beautiful smile,
have slowly been changing, for now quite a while.
Those pearly white teeth, now dingy and brown,
with many replaced, with a bridge or a crown.
But don't give up hope, she can still save the day,
the dentist has tricks, if you're willing to pay.
And the sags and the wrinkles, they also will fade,
if a good plastic surgeon, will practice his trade.

And the extra few pounds, build up over years,
just eat fewer calories, and it all disappears.

Politics

By the people, for the people, a well-known written line,
if this described our government, our country would be fine.
Most people who we now elect, have good ideas at first,
then power becomes the only thing, for which they strongly thirst.
All the things they used to say, words that got them elected,
appear to now have been forgotten, or the idea just rejected.
What they said when they campaigned, the truth or just an act?
now all they hear is their party's voice, and obediently react.
Were their early words sincere, or uttered with a wink?
'cause now what their party says, is the only way they think.
We really wanted something good, they knew what we expected,
the promises they made have gone, as usual we're neglected.
Immediate action must be taken, wake up and sound the alarm.
Go to the polls and vote them out before they do more harm.

Relief

I'm gonna tell you a story, and I'll try to be brief,
and the tale that I tell you, is about man's relief.
When early man had to go, he went out in the woods,
there he simply squatted down, and deposited his goods.
This went on for many years, until somebody found,
a better solution was to dig, a deep hole in the ground.
Far away from their cave, the hole was always placed,
so odors couldn't reach them, from all the smelly waste.
Gradually people got relief, from privies out in back,
all deposits now were made, afar in a wooden shack.
It had a seat with a hole, and a half moon on the door,
all deposits in the hole, dropped beneath the floor.
Fancier folk, not used to this, and being far less bold,
didn't want to make deposits, outside in the cold.
They found a way to get relief, right next to their cot,
they simply put beside their beds, a great big chamber pot.
Later came a real smart man, John was his first name,
his last name I don't recall, my memory has gone lame.
But John made a toilet, it actually worked and flushed,
when you jerked upon a chain, the water really gushed.

Relief (Continued...)

John's toilet worked like he said, but didn't work very well,
everything flushed down the drain, but it still left the smell.
When a person seeks relief, there're smells they really hate,
smells left over when a toilet's flushed, folks won't tolerate.
John tried everything he knew, to make the smells abate,
when nothing worked his smelly toilet, met a dismal fate.
Others tried for many years, to find another way,
and finally came Tom Krapper, he really saved the day.
In Krapper's toilet, pull the chain, it flushes very well,
everything is down the drain, along with the awful smell.
But Krapper's toilet good as it was, didn't help very much,
many folks continued using, pots and holes and such.
Krapper's great creation, was ignored by the masses,
I guess they just liked smelling, the odors and the gasses.
Still today in foreign countries, it's far beyond belief,
they squat right in the gutters, of their streets to get relief.
But here at home where we live, the toilets are really neat,
some will flush without our help, and have a padded seat.
What the future holds for toilets, is really hard to tell,
one thing that we know for sure, they're not going to smell.

Grit

I've heard many people ask, just what is a grit?
A grit's part of a kernel of corn, a tiny little bit.
This tiny grain tastes real good, breakfast or at lunch,
but you have to eat lots of them, combined as a bunch.
Just scoop up a spoonful, put them on your plate,
and the taste that you experience, really is first rate.
If you are a Southerner, and grew up in the South,
a spoonful of grits, will melt right in your mouth.
Eatin' breakfast in the South, a person always gits,
usually eggs, a slice of ham, but always lots of grits.
You can eat grits by itself, but usually it's all mixed,
it always tastes really good, no matter how it's fixed.
You can mix it up with eggs, or any kind of meat,
you can eat it when it's cold, or give it some heat.
You can put cheese in it, or mix it up with fish,
no matter how you fix it, it's still a real good dish.
If you let it get real cold, it will get real hard,
then you can fry it, in grease or in some lard.
Most folks will never try it, outside of the South,
to us it's like dessert, and melts right in your mouth.

Heroes

Our heroes of the years gone by, were mostly not too bad.
they defended all the weak, with everything they had.
They helped out both young and old, showed them much respect,
children and the weaker sex, they always would protect.
They never had too much to drink, and they never lied,
they never stole and didn't cheat, by the laws they did abide.
They didn't use illegal drugs, and never did they cuss,
they were great role models, for all the kids like us.
Our world today has changed a lot, now the things we see,
is little concern for anyone, now it's all about me.
Just look at the heroes, our kids have today,
rich and famous athletes, our laws they don't obey.
They have children here and there, usually with no wife,
these little kids have little chance, to have a normal life.
They punch and slap their girlfriends, as well as their wives,
and sometimes in a fit of anger, even take their lives.
It isn't just the athletes, who set the bad examples,
many famous actors, can easily serve as samples.
Heavy use of alcohol, and drugs that they abused,
leaves their bodies in a wreck, their minds a bit confused.
Out of wedlock they have kids, this is really sad,

Heroes (Continued...)

mothers with no morals, and God knows who's their dad.
There're also politicians, our young folks sometimes see,
as a person they admire, and like to grow up to be.
But sometimes politicians, the same ones they admire,
are all too often cheaters, and sometimes too a liar.
Many heroes of the present, are really second rate,
their behavior our kids see, and sometimes emulate.
Many role models of today, should really be ashamed,
if our kids do the things they do, they should not be blamed.
Heroes our kids have today, with whom they identify,
set real bad examples, and that you can't deny.
Many of the heroes our kids see, are a pretty sorry lot,
their behavior our kids copy, that's all that they have got.
Sometimes people appear to be good, and this is really sad,
'cause often folks who seem real good, turn out really bad.
Good role models do exist, and sometimes can be found,
just look for people doing good, and they are around.
It's rare they get a headline, or appear on TV news,
and rarely will you see them, bragging in interviews.
Their behavior's usually subtle, not seen by everyone,
but they continue to help others, until the job is done.

Sickly

I was sittin' 'round, just thinkin' the other day,
how my friends' health, is quickly going away.
As the years pass by, and old age is drawing near,
they have all these ailments, that start to appear.
They don't sleep well, as you think they might,
'cause they keep waking up, to pee thru the night.
And at about forty, most always seem to need,
to start wearing glasses, if they want to read.
And if they want, to get their vision back,
usually requires some surgery, for a cataract.
I also notice, most things they can't hear,
without a hearing aid, stuck in their ear.
I have to always shout, from not real far away,
for them to hear, what I have to say.
And sometimes their heart, doesn't work right,
it loses its rhythm, beats fast day and night.
The reason for this, has an explanation,
what it's called is, Atrial Fibrillation.
If they eat good things, like steak and such,
they get the Gout, from eatin' it too much.
Also eatin' steaks, and good food like that,
clogs up their arteries, with big blobs of fat.

That makes them all ready, for a heart attack,
but just get a stent or two, they're back on track.
Many have bad backs, they can't twist or dip,
some also have other aches, in a knee or a hip.
And with age their libido, I've heard does decline,
but just take a Viagra, and things will be just fine.
But with all these problems, they still do OK,
by acting like a twenty, year old every day.

Geriatrics

Those nearing retirement, frequently have fear,
doing nothing all day, they simply can't bear.
Now I'm all retired, and I'm busy all day,
I never have a moment, to do nothing or play.
An appointment book, I must keep in sight,
to not forget appointments, just like I might.
Monday to the gym, then off to Walmart,
I need spark plugs, so my mower will start.
Then to a doctor's, appointment at three,
to find out what's wrong, with my hurting knee.
Early Tuesday the dentist, then golf I will play,
then a couple of beers, and my golf bets I pay.
It's Wednesday morning, and I'm back at the gym,
gotta keep my body, real fit and trim.
A quick lunch and I'm off, to the doctor's again.
the dermatologist's freezin', some things off my skin.
Now on Thursday morning, I'm out before eight,
to my ophthalmologist, don't want to be late.
From there I head, to the local drug store,
I've got lots of meds, but I've got to get more.
With my pills now in hand, everything will be fine,
so I head downtown, to meet friends for wine.

Geriatrics (Continued...)

Now it's Friday morning, it's the gym once more,
to pump some iron, get my muscles all sore.
Friday afternoon's my, cardiologist's day,
hopefully my heart's, still pumping away.
He'll check my heart, prescribe another pill,
then back to the drug store, to get them a fill.
When I used to work, before retirement came,
my life now seems, to be just the same.
I used to spend my time, doing things required,
and it seems the same, now that I'm retired.
I still have to wait, for a weekend day,
to not be real busy, and have time to play.

Happy

Some folks are unhappy, and it could be you,
if you want to stay happy, what should you do?
Some go and play cards, some others go fishin',
others like to gamble, and do lots of wishin'.
Some enjoy tennis, or a good golf game,
but some see these things, as being right lame.
As the years pass by, and you get a bit older,
you look for a pastime, a little less bolder,
Your card playing partners, get fixed in their ways,
and fishin' ain't catchin', on most of the days.
Tennis will give, your elbow some pain,
besides that you, can't play in the rain.
And golf makes you hurt, usually in the back,
and the skills it takes, most of us lack.
Now gambling and betting, can often be fun,
but the odds of winning, are slim to none.
So what should we do, as the years pass us by?
On what kind of pleasures, can we rely?
We could sit in a chair, for an afternoon nap,
with some boring book, laying in our lap.
But wait! I'm inspired! I have an idea!
Something we can do, that we'd like I hear.

We can go to a movie, I'm sure there's one near,
what film is playing, we don't really care.
We get us some popcorn, and a big soft drink,
find a comfortable seat, sit in it and sink.
This leads to the part, of this I like best,
two uninterrupted hours, of dozing and rest.

Changes

Our life is in phases, and it seems very strange,
the things that we value, constantly change.
All we want as an infant, are hugs and some food,
and a clean dry diaper, will change our mood.
When we get in our teens, we get real bright,
our parents get dumber, and never are right.
Me and my friends, we knew everything,
with no thought of what, our actions might bring.
Later we're married, the first years are bliss,
but later things sometimes, they go all amiss.
The joy that we saw, in those early years,
is replaced by fighting, and shouting and tears.
To escape all this yelling, shouting and fighting,
we turn to another, who looks more inviting.
Our marriage will end, 'cause sometimes we stray,
and one of the partners, goes some other way.
This usually brings, a big change in life,
and sometimes a brand new, husband or wife.
As the years keep passing, and old age is near,
our opinions get stronger, we're hard to bear.
Our waistlines grow out, way over our lap,
and each afternoon, we need a short nap.

But the one change in life, that we'll never see,
no matter what happens, I'll still be me.

Wormy

While on my way home, the other night,
I saw something sad, off to the right.
Little fake flowers, and large head stones,
gave me a chill, right down to my bones.
A big cemetery, was what I was seein',
and that ain't a place, I look forward to bein'.
The folks buried there, don't have any fun,
just lyin' underground, away from the sun.
They have no company, 'cept worms and bugs,
nobody to talk to, or give them some hugs.
It made me think, just how lucky we are,
we can go to a restaurant, or maybe a bar.
We can have us a meal, or a good glass of wine,
'cause we're above ground, where the sun does shine.
And other live people, are sitting around,
and they like me too, are all above ground.
Good company and friends, is what one expects,
not under the ground, with the worms and insects.

Transfiguration

Have you ever thought, how strange it would be,
if your body wasn't like, what we usually see.
If your ears were moved, from the side of your head,
and then placed down, on your buttocks instead.
Now when you sit, with your weight on your rear,
would you still hear things. like you normally hear?
And if your nose, was turned upside down,
stay out of the rain, 'cause you'll likely drown.
And what if your eyes, were moved to the back,
and the front of your face, now eyes did lack.
In the past where you're going, you could easily see,
but now you see only, where you used to be.
And what would happen, if your lips made a change,
and moved under your chin, wouldn't that look strange?
Now anything to drink, you would have to decline,
or lay on your back, to drink whiskey or wine.
Since none of this happened, my body's intact,
still perfect as ever, and that is a fact.

Naggy

A poor husband's work, is never done,
he keeps gettin' jobs, he ain't finished none.
His honey-do list, just grows and grows,
how big it will get, no one really knows.
He's even given jobs, as he watches TV,
if he does these jobs, the screen he can't see.
And his afternoon nap, is often in doubt,
'cause he's being nagged, to take the trash out.
Why can't a wife, share with these chores?
She has lots of time, after sweeping the floors.
All she does all day, is some cleaning and cook,
and interrupt me, while I read a book.
Then she sits at her desk, paying the bills,
she probably does that, just for the thrills.
Doing laundry and ironing, makes her pout,
but my clothes should look good, when I go out.
And she's slow sometimes, in getting me fed,
and wants me to help her, make up the bed.
With all her free time, you'd think that she,
would do more chores, and just let me be.
I remember last night, she continued to whine,
as I asked her to bring me, a glass of red wine.

All she was doing, was cleaning and cooking,
and I was real busy, at TV I was looking.

Birdy

How awful the life, of a bird must be,
spending all day, in the top of a tree.
Only leaving occasionally, to fly around,
to look for a worm, down on the ground.
I wouldn't like it much, I really must say,
just eating bugs, and worms every day.
When winter arrives, and the temperature falls,
their nests don't have heat, don't even have walls.
And when the rains come, their feathers will try,
to block the raindrops, but they still won't stay dry.
But I'm not a bird, I'm happy to say,
and don't have to live, in a tree every day.

Timely

As I awakened, was it seven or eight?
I need to know, so I won't be late.
Did the clock spring forward, or did it fall back?
Is it time for me, to get out of the sack?
This time of the year, I'm really enthused,
one hour more sleep, but my body's confused.
It says get up, but that shouldn't be,
the clock and my body, just don't agree.
We've had this time change, many times before,
Ben Franklin first did it, 1864.
He said our clocks, should follow the sun,
but he made this suggestion, just for fun.
Saving candle wax, was his stated intent,
but folks didn't know, just what he meant.
And the time change stayed, never went away,
and it looks like forever, it's going to stay.
Daylight Savings Time, with me is OK,
but I'm always confused, on the time of the day.

Richy

My day has come, I'm gonna be wealthy!
My bank account's gonna, soon get real healthy.
'Cause I got an e-mail, the other day,
I was happy but shocked, by what it did say.
A lady from Somalia, who I did not know,
offered me a deal, to make my cash grow.
She's the heiress in a very, rich man's will,
whose estate is worth, about twenty mill.
She wants the funds moved, into the U.S.,
'cause in Somalia, they're worth much less.
But she needs a sponsor, over here to use,
so she made me an offer, I couldn't refuse.
If to be her sponsor, I would agree,
she'd split the whole, inheritance with me.
She said to make sure, that I didn't back out,
a thousand bucks, would remove any doubt.
So I wrote her a check, sent it right away,
and my ten million bucks, should arrive any day.
When I get my millions, here's what I think,
I'll buy my friends, all the wine they can drink.

Mental

I sometimes wonder, watching people all day,
are they acting normal, are their minds astray?
Some claim every illness, many and bad,
they've got everything, that could ever be had.
Are their ailments real, are they really a fact?
Or is it all in their mind, a Hypochondriac?
And some people think, that they are the goal,
of everything bad, that will ever unfold.
Everything's against them, things they can't avoid,
could this just be the thinking, of a true Paranoid?
A defense mechanism, we all sometimes use,
is Rationalization, which we use to excuse.
If we're bad at some skill, or commit a no no,
Rationalization's a good way, to save our ego.
And some people seem, so happy today,
but tomorrow their mood, is the other way.
Had something happened, to make them depressed?
Or are they Bipolar, this is how it's expressed.
And your partner's affection, you no longer seek,
it might be because, your Libido is weak.
My last thought about, why people act strange,
Senility might be, the cause of this change.

As our brain cells die, it's real hard to think,
we assist in this, by the booze that we drink.
So how's a real normal, person to be?
As a perfect example, just look at me.

Observation

I was having a beer, at a local bistro,
and was treated that day, to a real good show.
Many ladies there, just didn't have an issue,
showing off an abundance, of adipose tissue.
Just to sit and observe, was the very best part,
it was just like you'd see, at the local Walmart.
The jeans that some wore, were much too tight,
it's a wonder they, can get in 'em each night.
Their breasts were real large, enhanced by much fat,
if they lost fifty pounds, their chests would be flat.
Now some of the girls, looked neat and real trim,
but it was hard to tell, if it's a her or a him.
Some dressed like a man, with a tiny little butt,
and instead of long hair, had a manly crew cut.
And just like some people, frequently choose,
their body was covered, with great big tattoos.
With some young folks, tattoos are the rage,
but they don't look too good, as they start to age.
Some got their tattoos, when younger and bolder,
but now they're starting, to get a bit older.
Their tattoos are drooping, and starting to fade,
and look different now, from the day they were made.

And also with age, girls' chins start to bag,
and their triple D chests, start showing some sag.
But the girls that I know, don't look like that,
and most of them, are certainly not fat.
And none have tattoos, that I'm able to see,
there're none on the girls, or the guys or on me.
Many girls are well shaped, like an old Coke bottle,
and could probably still, be a high fashion model.
So if you want a beer, want to see a great show,
just meet me downtown, at the local bistro.

Feet-ish

The ugliest part, of today's human being,
are their ugly feet, hardly worth seeing.
Another reason I don't, like feet too well,
some have a rather, unpleasant smell.
And with toes sometimes, all gnarly and bent,
they don't ventilate well, this adds to the scent.
And those who wear sandals, just don't give a hoot,
they display corns and bunions, and blisters to boot.
And along with their sandals, socks some do wear,
how stupid they look, but they don't seem to care.
Some toenails are ugly, 'cause they haven't been cut,
from the end of their toes, out too far they jut.
Now overweight girls, with their fat little feet,
sometimes wear shower shoes, trying to look neat.
They hope that these shoes, will hide their fat toes,
and their ugly fat feet, they will not expose.
But their fat feet mash, their shoe soles down flat,
and their toes still look, like little blobs of fat.
But most girls nowadays, always polish their toes,
hiding parts of their feet, that add to their woes.
I'm hoping that today, no feet I will see,
in shoes or under tables, I hope they will be.

Sustenance

Many ages ago, when man first did arrive,
he required food and drink, just to survive.
He had no way to know, what's bad or good,
no labels to tell him, like on today's food.
The first thing he tried, the first thing he did see,
just as you might guess, he drank his own pee.
He was quick to realize, he needed food too,
so he tried what was closest, he tried his own poo.
This might seem pretty, stupid to some,
but that's where the term, "Copra Phagic" comes from.
He then looked for something, that's better to eat,
so he clubbed a Pterodactyl, and ate all his meat.
He searched for more food, caught a fish this time,
it was real hard to eat, because of the slime.
In the river he found, some shells he did get,
he opened them and saw, something gooey and wet.
He almost threw up, with the thing that he saw,
he became the first person, to eat oysters raw.
He searched for other, things he could eat,
found coons and rats, were real hard to beat.
He then picked some berries, let them sit for days,
ate them after they warmed, in the sun's rays.

The now fermented berries, which he had found,
made him giddy and dizzy, passed out on the ground.
With my eating habits, I'm sure I'll be fine,
I'll just eat some nuts, followed up with some wine.

Mysteries

The mysteries of life, I've constantly pondered,
how do things work, I've always wondered.
How do fish get into, ponds everywhere,
when I'm sure nobody, ever put them there.
And how does a ship, get into a bottle,
and it's fully complete, a real perfect model.
And what came first, the chicken or egg,
for the answer to this, I'd kneel down and beg.
For millennia now science, has been real involved,
trying to figure out, how humans evolved.
And the Missing Link question, still ain't understood,
if it was I'd explain it, but I doubt that I could.
Besides these mysteries, there are plenty more,
and their explanations, I'd like to explore.
But these great mysteries, I'll just let them be,
let somebody else, get the answers for me.
Getting these answers, will be really tough,
and I realize that, I just ain't smart enough.

The End

www.ingramcontent.com/pod-product-compliance
Lightning Source LLC
Chambersburg PA
CBHW071456030726
47593CB00003B/1028